AF413639

iSoldier

PINK

PINK: <u>P</u>icking <u>I</u>s <u>N</u>ot <u>K</u>ind

Picky Picky Perfect

written by

Becca Robinson

Picky, picky, perfect and I feel like a wreck.
Do it this way, do it that way, all these voices
in my head making my chest feel tight.

How can I ever be perfect if I can't see my light?
Always too busy being perfect and right.

Do it this way and do it that way and if I don't do it just right, I will be up all night.

I like everything in its spot.
That way I can stay on the dot.

But that dot, dot, dot keeps tying me in knots, knots, knots.

I must rethink its picky, picky pink cause
it keeps making me want to shrink.

Picky, picky, perfect, collect this,
protect that. Pick, pick, and peck,
peck now I feel like a defect.

Oh, you picky pink, let's sit
still a minute and think.

How can I get you from
picky to pretty?

To keep me in sync
and not sink.

I have battled before, and I now battle again
it's time to suit up and find the missing link.

I stand up and grab my helmet, knowing
that picky, picky, pink is not kind; and
remind myself no one is perfect all the time.

Wait, wait, wait.

No one is perfect, that's right no one is perfect!

BAM!

Just like that the pressure to look perfect stops clickety-clack.

Free from pressure yes this is me, I grab my breastplate
and start to release this picky, pick, pink.

I place my belt of truth around my belly and
detect that picky, picky, pink.

I pick up my shield and press this pink.
I am learning to deflect that picky pink.

With my sword in hand, I am on the
brink of breaking this picky pink.

I grab my boots and uproot that picky
pink and all its slimy stink.

Prayer, yes prayer is my ink that
will rewrite this picky pink.

I bow my head and kneel searching
my heart, perfect this and perfect
that where did you even start?

Oh, let me think I know there
must be pretty in this pink.

LOVE

Love allows me to disconnect
from picky, picky, pink and wink
at the pretty in the pink.

Helmet: Rethink the PINK
from picky to pretty.

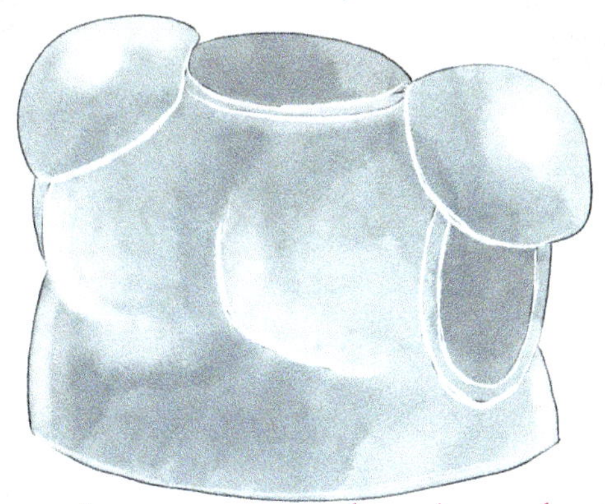

Breastplate: Don't shrink in the
PINK no hurtful picky words.

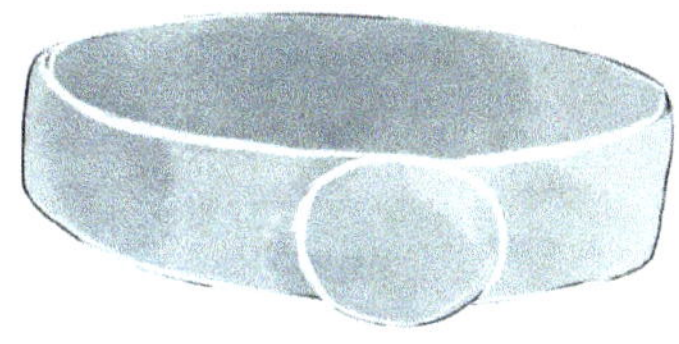

Belt: As I tighten my belt it
shrinks the picky PINK.

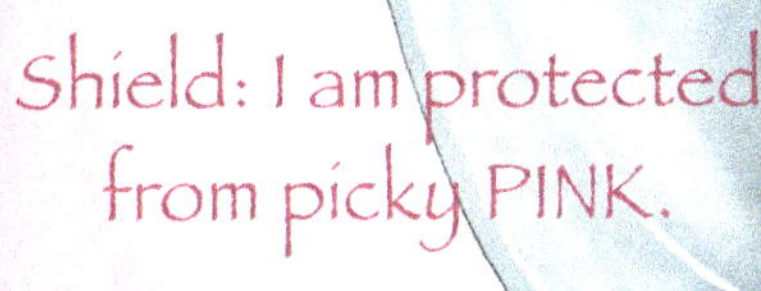

Shield: I am protected
from picky PINK.

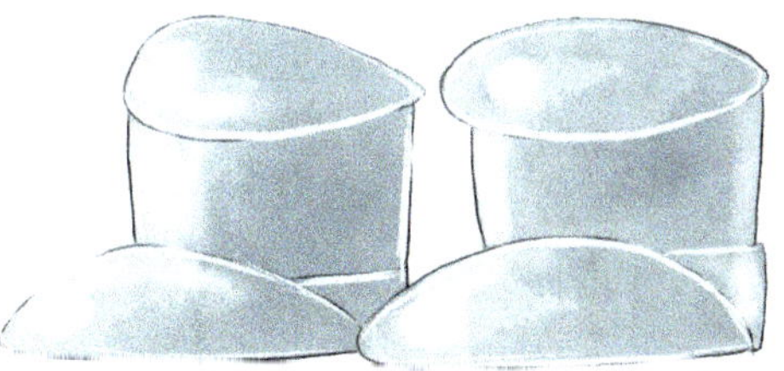

Boots: Roots, roots, roots, no
tangled picky tricky roots for me.

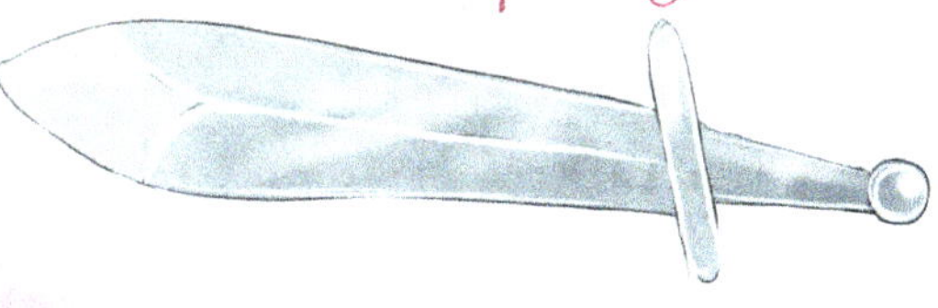

Sword: Cut away this picky
and see the pretty.

Prayer 1: John 4:18   Thank you, Jesus, for showing me that the only thing that can be perfect is perfect LOVE! Perfect love casts out all fear. If I am picking, I am not seeing perfect love.

I must look through LOVE to see the pretty and not be picking. That I'm made perfect in perfect Love.

Other Available Titles:

iSoldier BLUE, iSoldier RED,
iSoldier GREEN

Coming Soon:

iSoldier YELLOW,
iSoldier TOO